8   2/99
  1 8
5/00

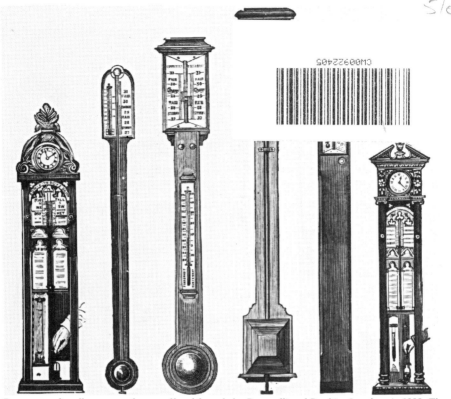

CM0092240S

Barometers for all: a range of types offered for sale by Pastorelli and Rapkin, London, in 1885. The firm supplied them to scientists and seamen, farmers and pitmen, householders rich and poor.

BAROMETERS

Anita McConnell

Shire Publications Ltd

CONTENTS

Published in 1998 by Shire Publications Ltd, Cromwell House, Church Street, Princes Risborough, Buckinghamshire HP27 9AA, UK. Website: www.shirebooks.co.uk

Copyright © 1988 by Anita McConnell. First published 1988; second edition 1994; reprinted 1998. Shire Album 220. ISBN 0 7478 0240 8.

All rights reserved. No part of this publication may be reproduced or transmitted in any form or by any means, electronic or mechanical, including photocopy, recording, or any information storage and retrieval system, without permission in writing from the publishers.

Printed in Great Britain by CIT Printing Services, Press Buildings, Merlins Bridge, Haverfordwest, Pembrokeshire SA61 1XF.

British Library Cataloguing in Publication Data: McConnell, Anita. Barometers. – 2 Rev. ed. – (Shire Albums; No. 220). I. Title. II. Series 681. ISBN 0 7478 0240 8.

ACKNOWLEDGEMENTS
Illustrations are acknowledged as follows: Patrick Marney, page 30; Science Museum, London (photographs by Michael Bass), pages 1, 4 (left), 5, 6 (left), 8 (top right and bottom), 9, 10, 11 (right), 12, 13 (left), 16, 19, 22 (bottom), 24, 25, 29 (left), 31, and front cover; Trustees of the National Museum of Scotland, page 23; Rosie Whicher, pages 4 (right), 6 (right), 11 (left), 14, 26, 29 (right).

Cover: *Diagonal barometer by Watkins and Smith, 1763, with spirit thermometer and hygrometer. The perpetual calendar in the centre panel shows dates of religious festivals and astronomical events from the year 1752, when Britain adopted the Gregorian calendar.*

Left: *Setting up a 'Torricellian experiment'. Illustration from a treatise on barometers, thermometers and hygrometers, published anonymously in 1688.*
Right: *Book frontispiece, 1753, showing an allegorical figure with a barometer tube. A thermometer can be seen on the wall.*

ORIGINS

The mercury barometer measures atmospheric pressure. It consists of a tube of mercury, sealed at the top and open to the air below. Air pressing on the open end supports a column of mercury whose weight is equal to that of the air pressure.

The atmosphere which envelopes our globe is held around the earth by gravity. The pull of gravity, which we feel and can measure as atmospheric pressure, decreases with height. At the top of Mount Everest atmospheric pressure is about half that at sea level. This pressure gradient is by no means uniform. The atmosphere is warmed by the sun in the day and cools at night. Its temperature is changed as it passes across warmer or colder lands and seas. Warm air rises whilst cold air sinks, and these vertical motions can overwhelm the basic pressure gradient and change the pressure that we measure at ground level. A glance at the sky usually shows that the air is moving horizontally as well, with clouds marking the speed and direction of winds high above our heads. These winds bring air of different temperatures, sometimes in calm, sometimes in stormy conditions, affecting pressure.

So the mercury barometer enables us to make 'absolute' pressure measurements, to measure altitude and to forecast the weather. It is surely one of the most useful inventions that science has given to mankind.

The barometer originated in seventeenth-century Florence. Philosophers in that city were debating the problem posed by Aristotle and his commentators: could a vacuum exist in nature? Meanwhile engineers responsible for draining mines wondered why their pumps and siphons could not raise water more than about 32 feet (10 metres). Eventually the men of science realised that the pumps might be creating a vacuum which prevented the water being raised higher.

To resolve these practical problems, several people set up experiments, among them Evangelista Torricelli, expert in hydraulics. His apparatus consisted of water in long pipes, and Torricelli found that the weather affected his experiments. He took the experiment indoors and substituted the heavier liquid mercury, so that he could use shorter pipes. In 1643 or 1644 (the exact date is disputed) he filled a tube with mercury and inverted it over a bowl of mercury. The mercury level fell a little way down the tube, then remained at a steady height of about 29 inches (73 centimetres). In tubes of equal diameter, 29 inches of mercury weighs the same as 32 feet of water.

Torricelli was able to prove that the empty space was indeed a vacuum. His simple arrangement (still known in schools as the 'Torricellian experiment') was effectively the first mercury barometer, though it did not receive this name until some years later.

News of this success soon spread through Italy. French philosophers eagerly copied and extended the experiment, and within a few years it was repeated in England. Besides confirming the existence of a vacuum, French physicists soon showed that the atmosphere exerted a pressure, higher at sea level than in the mountains. The Royal Society, from its inception in London in 1660, encouraged practical experiments and many of its members kept records of their barometer readings, which changes in the weather affected in some as yet unexplained way.

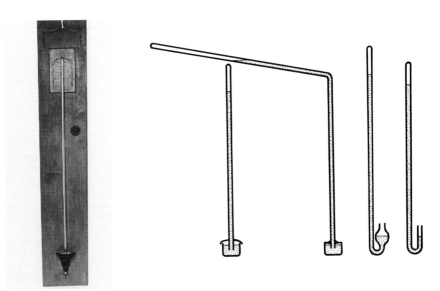

Left: *A simple tube-and-bowl barometer. A London barometer maker, Somalvico, made this reconstruction for his own collection.*
Right: *Alternatives to the open bowl: (left to right) bowl and lid; closed boxwood cistern, shown here with a diagonal tube; bottle tube; siphon tube.*

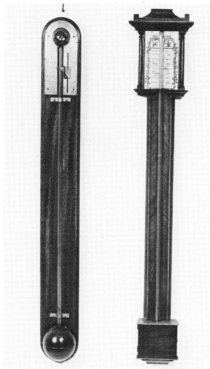
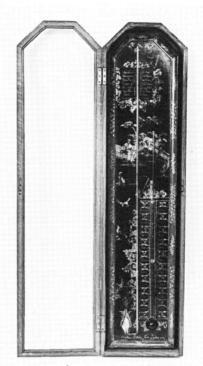

Left: *Two stick barometers. (Left) By Ramsden, about 1770. The tube is an early form, with an upper globe; the bowl has a loose lid. (Right) Bottle barometer by Manticha, about 1800. The scale plate is decorated with masonic symbols.*
Right: *Bottle barometer, with spirit thermometer, made by Isaac Robelou in 1719. The backboard is painted in Chinese style.*

BAROMETERS FOR THE HOME

Within a few years of Torricelli's work, the barometer had developed from a temporary assemblage of glassware and mercury to a fixed instrument, and could be found in the house of any gentleman with pretensions to learning.

The simple tube-and-bowl was not satisfactory as a permanent instrument because the mercury soon became dirty and did not slide easily along the tube. During the later seventeenth century four alternative forms were designed, which have remained in use. They may be seen today in barometers of all ages and in the replicas which are still popular.

The desired measurement is always the height of mercury in the tube *from the surface of mercury in the cistern.* The cistern level rises and falls as more or less mercury is drawn into the tube. With large cisterns the variation is small and for domestic barometers it is generally ignored.

The simplest way of keeping dirt out of the mercury was to put a loose-fitting lid over the bowl. A better idea was to seal the tube into a porous wood or leather container. The 'bottle' barometer, in which the tube is bent back, ending in a small bottle with a tiny hole to admit air pressure, is a variant on this idea. The sealed cistern and the bottle prevent

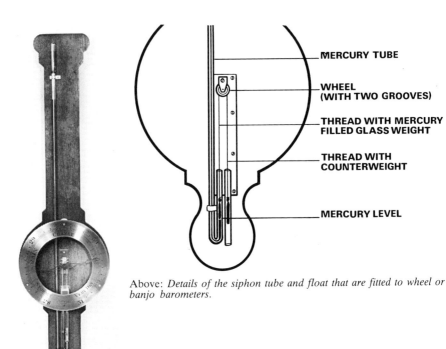

MERCURY TUBE

WHEEL
(WITH TWO GROOVES)

THREAD WITH MERCURY
FILLED GLASS WEIGHT

THREAD WITH
COUNTERWEIGHT

MERCURY LEVEL

Above: *Details of the siphon tube and float that are fitted to wheel or banjo barometers.*

Left: *Nineteenth-century demonstration model of a wheel barometer, made by Negretti and Zambra.*

accurate measurement of the height of the mercury column, but the glassware was cheap and easy to make. Small brass scale plates, covering the expected range of movement, often had pointers that could be set to previous readings, thus allowing comparison with the present.

Closed cistern and bottle forms may be cased as what is known as 'stick' barometers. For the most costly examples, cabinet-makers used exotic woods from the Caribbean and Far East to create beautiful pieces of furniture, veritable harmonies of art and science.

The 'wheel' barometer is commonly ascribed to Robert Hooke, who was demonstrator to the Royal Society in its early years. He illustrated it in 1664 and it has remained virtually unchanged since that time. Hooke's barometer had a large globe at the top of the tube, but later barometers do not have this feature. The mercury level in the lower limb responds to pressure change. A thread, running from a float on this surface, passes over a pulley and is balanced by a weight. A pointer attached to the pulley moves round the 'wheel'. With this arrangement, small changes in the mercury level are magnified by the pointer moving round a dial fixed to the wheel.

This expansion of the scale and the decorative shape (it became known as the 'banjo') combined to make this the cheapest and most popular type throughout the years. Wheels of 8 inches (20 cm) diameter were not out of place in modest rooms, whilst 10 or 12 inch (25 or 30 cm), or even larger, wheels were more in keeping with grand houses, where their readings were visible from a distance.

Dirt and dust can get into the open tube of a wheel barometer. After some years the mercury corrodes and the reading is sluggish and inaccurate. The strings rot and must be replaced. Maintenance is essential if the barometer is to be relied on.

There are few places in the world where pressure varies annually by more than 4 inches (equivalent to 135 millibars). In temperate lands the daily change is usually less than an inch (34 mb). In earlier centuries, when hand-blown barometer tubes were somewhat irregular in bore, these small changes were hardly visible. In consequence, ingenious minds devised ways to increase the distance over which the mercury travelled, so that the smallest variation might be observed.

The wheel barometer, mentioned above, expanded the scale according to the length of its pointer. With 'folded' and 'diagonal' barometers the glass tube itself was lengthened. Several types of folded barometer were contrived in the seventeenth century, the most successful being designed by Amontons in 1688. He folded the tube into three limbs, with mercury in the cistern, then a lighter liquid, then another mercury sector, and a final capping of light liquid which extended past the scale. Lighter liquids,

Hicks of Hatton Garden, London, sold wheel barometers to suit all Victorian tastes. Note the elaborate spiral-bulb thermometers, a deliberately 'antique' feature.

49.   50.   51.

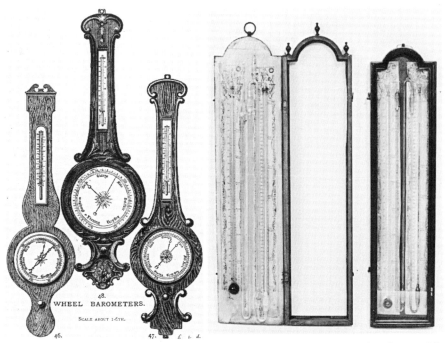

Left: *Even the owners of modest homes could afford a simple wheel barometer such as these models, offered for sale in the latter half of the nineteenth century.*
Right: *Two folded barometers made by Manticha and by Sala, both of London. On the left of each panel is a spirit thermometer. The barometer tubes are undamaged but empty.*

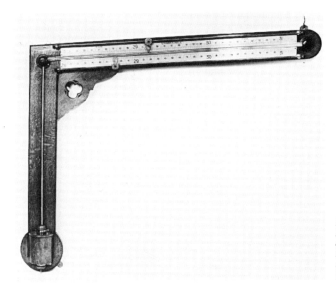

Diagonal barometer by Negretti and Zambra, about 1880. The mercury travels 12 inches along the diagonal arm for every 1 inch vertical rise or fall.

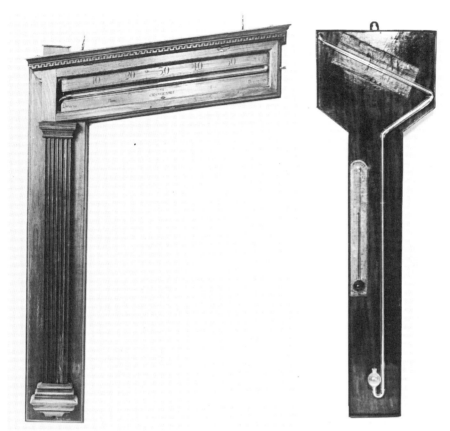

Left: *A diagonal barometer made around 1770 for King George III by Joseph Finney, a noted Liverpool clockmaker.*
Right: *Reticulated bottle barometer by Balthazar Knie of Edinburgh, about 1800. Knie made a speciality of these neat angled barometers.*

as Torricelli realised when experimenting with water, move further than mercury when pressure changes. The inventors of such multiple barometers hoped, by a judicious combination of fluids, to achieve sensitive yet compact instruments. In practice, however, great skill was demanded of the glass-blower. The quantity of each liquid was critical and the lighter liquid collected dirt and evaporated from the open end. Thus sensitivity was soon lost whilst the entire instrument was expensive to make and extremely fragile. Nevertheless, some examples have survived, usually incomplete.

The upper portion of a diagonal barometer is bent so that the mercury travels past several inches of scale for each inch gained in height. The principle is straightforward, but again the tube is difficult to blow and the increased friction as the elongated mercury surface travels along the tube makes it slow to respond to change. However, if the tube was set in a decorative frame it made a most impressive piece of furniture, its attraction outweighing its performance.

PORTABLE BAROMETERS

The barometers mentioned so far were never intended to be moved. Yet, once they suspected that atmospheric pressure decreased with height, physicists were taking barometers up mountains and down mines, looking for the relationship between pressure and altitude. The 'Torricellian experiment' was portable. Its tubes, bowl, mercury and ruler were carried separately and reassembled for each observation. This was commonly done well into the eighteenth century. Among the icy peaks, it was no easy matter to set up the apparatus, nor to keep the tubes and mercury clean and dry, although the work could be made easier by carrying spare tubes already filled and plugged.

Daniel Quare, who made clocks and barometers for royalty, patented a portable barometer in 1695. In those days patents were granted without details being supplied, so Quare's invention remains uncertain. Evidence suggests that his tubes were narrowed at the top, so that the barometers could safely be moved. Quare and his contemporaries also made cisterns of leather, which could be compressed by a screw. Under compression, mercury filled the tube and the barometer could then be safely carried at any angle. When the screw was released, the vacuum reappeared. The leather cistern was fitted to various types of barometer and, like most simple ideas, has much to commend it. Accuracy is limited, as the level of mercury in the cistern is not visible.

Around 1755 De Luc fitted a tap into the siphon barometer, to retain the mercury and thus make it portable. The arrangement was not as neat as Quare's but had the merit of allowing the surveyor to make accurate measurements, as both levels of mercury could be seen.

During the eighteenth and nineteenth centuries no expedition worthy of the name departed without one or more barometers in its luggage. At the summit of Mont Blanc, Europe's highest mountain, pressure is barely 17 inches (576 mb); in the Andes and Himalayas it falls much lower. The mountain barometer, therefore, needs a longer scale than its

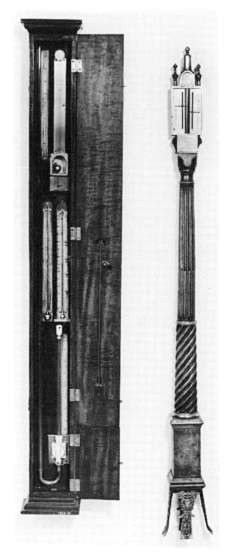

Portable barometers. (Left) De Luc's type, made by Nairne in about 1770. The barometer was set up vertically with the aid of the plumb-bob seen at the upper right. (Right) Portable barometer by Daniel Quare, about 1700.

10

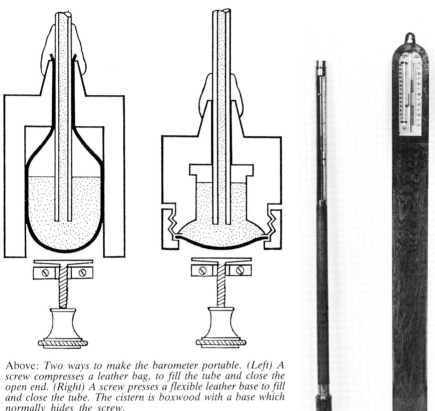

Above: *Two ways to make the barometer portable. (Left) A screw compresses a leather bag, to fill the tube and close the open end. (Right) A screw presses a flexible leather base to fill and close the tube. The cistern is boxwood with a base which normally hides the screw.*

Right: *On the left is a portable mountain barometer invented by Sir Henry Englefield in 1808. A wooden case protects the mercury tube. On the right is a pit, or miner's, barometer, with a plain and sturdy case and a scale ranging from 27 to 33 inches.*

domestic relatives and its cistern must be roomy enough to contain the falling mercury. Much effort went into calculating tables to convert pressure to altitude before physicists realised that the relationship was far from simple.

The first mountain barometers, and the similarly portable survey barometers, were heavy instruments. The noted English maker Jesse Ramsden designed a barometer with its own tripod, weighing 6 pounds (2.7 kg). Hurter designed a barometer plus tripod in 1786 which weighed less than Ramsden's; Englefield designed an even lighter travelling stick barometer, but without a tripod.

To provide a barometer which was robust, yet lightweight, instrument makers fitted fine-bore tubes (which were stronger yet held less mercury) into slender brass cases. When the Fortin barometer, with its glass cistern, was taken as the basis for a mountain barometer, the result was an extremely accurate instrument, well adapted for the most demanding survey operations.

Barometers for use below ground must have the scale extended to register higher pressures. In Britain, 'pit barometers' were taken down coal mines to detect changes in pressure caused by escaping gas.

11

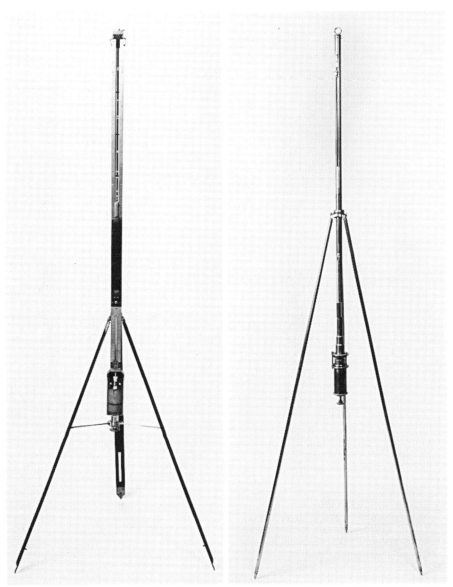

Left: *Portable mountain barometer as designed by Hurter in 1786, with a wooden case and boxwood cistern. Its hinged tripod folds upwards round the barometer when it is carried. A plumb-bob and thermometer are on the front of the case.*

Right: *This slender brass-cased Fortin barometer by Leroy, Paris, has the long scale and large cistern needed for mountain surveys where the mercury column might fall to 20 inches (50 cm) or less.*

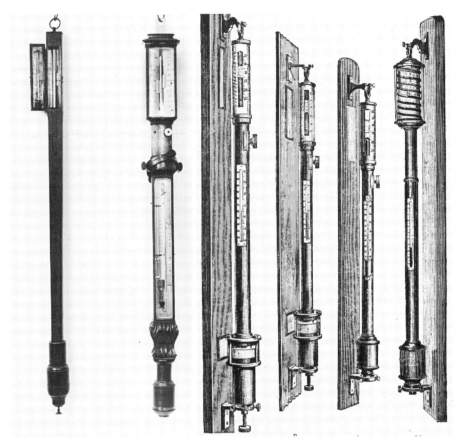

Left: *Two early nineteenth-century marine barometers in wooden cases. The decorative barometer on the right has a gimbal ring to support it on board ship and a sympiesometer on the case.*
Right: *Late nineteenth-century standard barometers were bought by scientific institutions and colleges, as well as private individuals. The two on the left have Fortin cisterns.*

Another form of portable barometer was needed on board ship. At sea, where rapid falls in pressure may herald approaching storms or cyclones, the barometer could save ships sailing into danger. The marine barometer had to be readable even in rough seas. To prevent the mercury surging in the tube as the vessel moved, the tube was given a narrow bore between the cistern and the scale. Hooke had suggested this feature in the 1660s, but the first evidence of its adoption is a century later. Unfortunately this constriction slowed down the mercury's descent when pressure fell sharply: the very condition that heralded storms.

Early nineteenth-century marine barometers had the main body made in wood, usually mahogany. The tube was cemented into a boxwood and leather cistern with adjusting screw, usually covered by a brass base. The barometers were mounted on gimbal fittings to counteract the rougher movements of the ship. Later versions, in their metal cases, have a more workmanlike appearance. Both patterns are commonly fitted with thermometers, for it was understood by then that the barometer's mercury expanded in warm weather, and a correction should be applied if readings from various places and times were to be truly

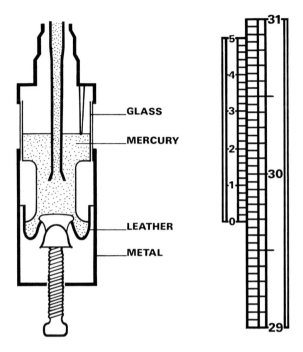

GLASS

MERCURY

LEATHER

METAL

Far left: *Fortin designed his cistern with glass sides so that the mercury could be adjusted to touch a fixed pointer, which marked the zero of the scale. 'Fortin' surveying and standard barometers have this or similar cisterns.*

Left: *With the vernier, a short, movable scale sliding against the main scale, observers could confidently measure the mercury column to fractions of an inch.*

comparable. Barometers on board ships in tropical or polar waters were naturally subject to extremes of temperature, unlike the domestic barometer.

As scientific and domestic barometers multiplied, it was essential to have a few especially well made examples, to act as standards. From these, instrument makers could calibrate their wares, and barometers in regular use could be checked from time to time. The Royal Society in London, and similar institutions elsewhere, therefore commissioned barometers from the best craftsmen of the day. A number of such old standards have survived the centuries, usually with their original owners, or in national collections. In Britain the term 'Standard' or 'Kew Standard' came to denote barometers checked at Kew Observatory, later the National Physical Laboratory.

In contrast to the rough and ready measurement shown by domestic banjo barometers, the observer reading a standard barometer can measure the exact height of the column, from the level in the cistern to the top of the meniscus, or

curve, in the tube. The reading is then corrected for temperature and for the barometer's height above sea level. The latter correction enabled barometer readings taken in different parts of the country to be compared. Typical features of a standard barometer are: an adjustable pointer which can be set to the level of mercury in the cistern at the moment of observation; a fine engraved scale, with a vernier and lens; and a thermometer set into the cistern. Nineteenth-century standards had wide-bore tubes, to reduce optical distortion and present a flatter surface of mercury to the observer. The present-day British Standard, housed in the National Physical Laboratory, operates under the most rigorous conditions, attended by electronic observers rather than the inefficient human eye.

When national observatories were established, mostly during the late eighteenth and early nineteenth centuries, fine, and often large, barometers were commissioned for what became long series of observations. Like the standards, such barometers survive in small numbers, mostly in the public domain.

At this point it seems appropriate to introduce the subject of scales, figures and words on barometers. So far inches have been used, because that is what we find on all barometers prior to the end of the eighteenth century. The standard inches of each country did vary slightly, and some barometer makers engraved more than one scale on the plates. French inches were generally divided into 12 'lines' while English inches were divided into tenths, but here and elsewhere exceptions are not rare.

The metric system, introduced by French law in 1801, slowly made its appearance on barometers but failed to displace inches entirely. Confusion reigned until the First World War, after which, by international agreement, scientists finally discarded a measurement that was merely the length of a mercury column. The standard unit of atmospheric pressure is now the 'bar', for convenience divided into 1000 'millibars', and these units are used throughout the world to-day. One bar corresponds to 29.53 inches of mercury.

Words on barometer scales are endlessly fascinating. Depending on the space available, makers set their name, address, some emblem or symbol, remarks on the expected height of the mercury in summer and winter and weather prognostications. Generally, the more 'serious' the instrument is, the fewer words are supplied (presumably scientists were expected to know what a falling barometer portended). The empty spaces on large banjo barometers tempted some engravers into an orgy of remarks, flourishes and even landscape vignettes. The materials that they had to work on became more diverse. In addition to the brass and paper scales fitted on the earliest barometers, nineteenth-century makers now offered silvered brass, ivory, ivorine and white glass, at greater or lesser prices.

KING'S SELF-RECORDING BAROMETER.

This instrument, the invention of Mr. ALFRED KING, Engineer of the Liverpool Gas Company, is in use at the Liverpool Observatory, where it yields results of a highly satisfactory character.

The accompanying Figure shows the relative positions of the various parts. A is the Barometer tube, made, in this instance, of steel, and having an internal diameter of three inches; it floats freely in the fixed cistern B, guided by friction wheels W. This tube is attached to a short-linked metal chain, which passes over a grooved wheel turning on finely adjusted friction rollers. The frame D is suspended, with its recording apparatus and weight, to the other end of the chain, and thus forms a counterpoise to the Barometer tube. The cylinder C is covered with ruled and divided tracing paper, and revolves *once in* 24 *hours*, thus producing the result

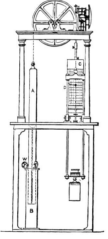

SCALE ABOUT 1-12TH.

described by Mr. HARTNUP, the Director of the Liverpool Observatory, who says:—" For one inch change in the mercurial column the pencil passes through five inches, so that the horizontal lines on the tracing, which are half an inch apart, represent 1-10th of an inch change in the Barometer. The vertical lines are hour lines and, being nearly three-quarters of an inch apart, it will be seen that the smallest appreciable change in the Barometer, and the time of its occurrence, are recorded."

The King barometer stood about 10 feet (3 metres) high. Several were made; the Liverpool Observatory instrument described here is now in Liverpool Museum.

15

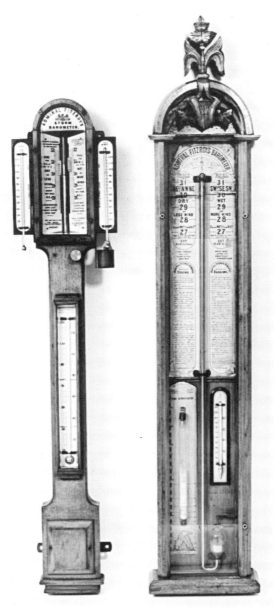

(Left) Fitzroy's storm barometer with wet and dry bulb thermometers. (Right) The domestic Admiral Fitzroy barometer has enjoyed more than a century of popularity and reproductions are still being made.

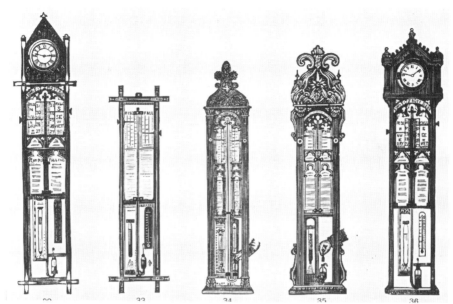

Fitzroy barometers to suit all tastes, from Casella's catalogue of 1908. Bottle tube, storm glass, thermometer and Fitzroy's Rules are the essential components; the rest depends on the customer's pocket.

WEATHER FORECASTING

By the nineteenth century a considerable number of barometer observations, made in homes, institutions and observatories in Europe, and to a lesser degree overseas, had accumulated. Yet the pattern of change, what we know today as weather systems, was not understood. This failing was due in part to the absence of regular timekeeping. Imagine the difficulty of trying to plot the movement of a gale, when each town kept its own local time. Yet, if some devastating storm raged across one or more countries and retained its identity, it was often possible to discover the pressure changes that had preceded, accompanied and followed it.

This analysis, depending on the postal system, could take many months, until, by the 1860s, weather reports within Europe and North America could be telegraphed, to reach central offices within hours. By charting the weather across the country at a given time, it was possible to identify the large- and small-scale pressure changes associated with settled weather, rain, storms and gales.

Forecasting became a realistic proposition and the barometer its principal tool.

Admiral Fitzroy, former naval hydrographer, established at the Board of Trade, forerunner of Britain's Meteorological Office, believed that many coastal fishing and cargo boats were lost each year when their captains put to sea unaware of approaching storms. He designed a 'fishery barometer', which by 1858 he had arranged to be displayed at each port, however small, to warn sailors of coming bad weather. Their large clear scales bear Fitzroy's 'Rules', forecasting the wind and weather to be expected from the barometer's tendency. Many of these barometers survive, still to be seen around the coasts of Britain in harbourmasters' offices and such places. Fitzroy provided similar rules for marine barometers, to be used in local waters. A 'farmers' barometer' was also made.

Fitzroy did not devise the other 'Fitzroy barometer', sold in vast numbers after his death and up to the present day, for they are still being made. The classic elements of this domestic barometer are: a bottle tube, a thermometer, a storm glass and Fitzroy's Rules.

The storm glass, familiar before Fitzroy's day, contains crystals of potassium nitrate and ammonium chloride dissolved in water, added to camphor dissolved in alcohol. Some instructions say that the tube should be loosely corked, others that it should be sealed. Feathery or granular crystals appear and disappear within the tube, apparently in response to temperature, wind and pressure changes, and the storm glass was believed to forecast the weather.

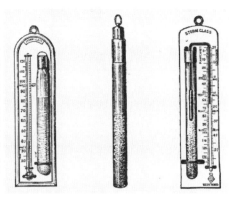

Storm glasses have been made and sold in Britain for more than two centuries. Until recently, particularly in seaside towns, some shopkeepers put up large glasses as advertising features.

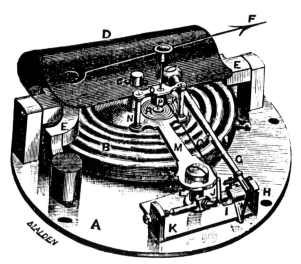

SCALE ABOUT 3-4THS.

The aneroid barometer. B is the corrugated vacuum box; D is its restoring spring. Other parts make up the linkage through which the tiny vertical movement of the box sides becomes the larger horizontal sweep of the pointer.

Aneroid barometers. (Centre) With curved mercury and spirit thermometers. (Right) Marine aneroid: the central diagram is the curve of normal sea-level pressure along the 30°W meridian.

ANEROID BAROMETERS

We now move from the mercury baro-meter to an instrument that even the humblest home could afford. The aneroid (the word means 'without liquid') was named by its French inventor Lucien Vidie. The demand for accurate steam gauges in the early nineteenth century led Vidie to his design, which was patented in 1844, and which he realised was equally applicable to measuring atmospheric pressure.

The sensing element of an aneroid is a flexible metal box, from which most of the air has been pumped. Changing air pressure compresses or relaxes this box and the movement is transmitted and magnified through a system of levers, ending in a pointer moving round the dial. The aneroid was calibrated with reference to a mercury barometer and was sometimes supplied with a crude temperature compensation.

Aneroid barometers were so cheap to make, lightweight and transportable that they immediately became popular. For the rich or *nouveau riche* Victorian householder the most elaborate cabinets were on offer; for the modest home,

factory or ship a simpler style; while for the traveller, the aneroid could be made small enough to fit a conventional watch-case.

Handy though it was, the aneroid was less accurate than a mercury barometer. Owing to the elastic properties of the metal used for the box, aneroids brought rapidly down from a height do not im-mediately read correctly. Manufacturers tried to remedy this defect either mecha-nically, or by putting 'ascending' and 'descending' scales on their dials, or by issuing printed correction tables.

The earliest aeronauts, having taken off before the aneroid was invented, had taken up siphon, Englefield or similar lightweight barometers within their bal-loon baskets. The Englefield is some-times now described as a 'balloon baro-meter' but not all examples have long enough scales to have been of any use aloft. 'Aviators' aneroids' were made to read down to 10 inches or the millibar equivalent. James Glaisher, in a series of balloon ascents made in 1862, compared aneroid and mercury siphon barometers down to 7 inches. Small portable aneroids

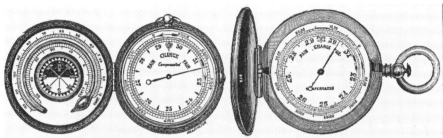

Fig. 43.   Fig. 45.

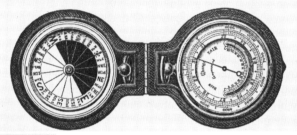

Above: *An aneroid barometer, with altitude scale, thermometer and compass, and fitted neatly into a pocket-watch case, was ideal for travelling gentlemen and mountaineers.*

Left: *A siphon-tube barometer made to draw its own record.*

Below: *The Victorian buyer could have his aneroid barometer, with or without clock and thermometer, encased to match his style of interior decoration.*

WATKIN ANEROID BAROMETER.

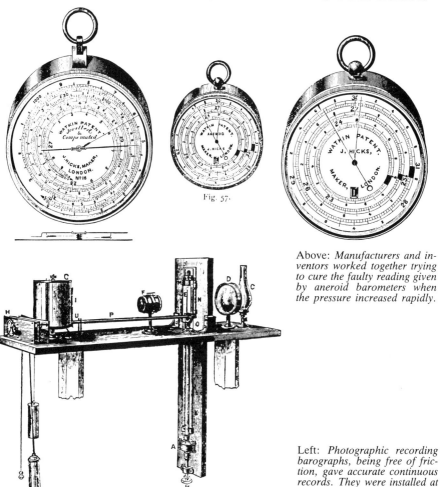

Fig. 57.

Above: *Manufacturers and inventors worked together trying to cure the faulty reading given by aneroid barometers when the pressure increased rapidly.*

Left: *Photographic recording barographs, being free of friction, gave accurate continuous records. They were installed at several British observatories.*

were taken on board by the first pilots, but these were soon adapted into purpose-made altimeters, where they remain a standard element in the aeroplane instrument panel.

As barometers became more accurate and the smallest changes in pressure were seen to be important in weather analysis and forecasting, the frequency of observations was stepped up. Eventually the barometer was made to record its own reading. At first, such 'barographs' were mechanical, operated by clockwork to make the pointer register at regular intervals. These primitive barographs, their records distorted by friction and necessarily crude, were set aside when, in the 1840s, photography found in the meteorological observatory one of its first industrial applications. Photography did not interfere with the instrument itself, no extra fittings being required. A tiny point of light shining across the mercury in a barometer tube could be continuously recorded on a moving strip of photosensitive paper, partnered by a time-trace. (The international acceptance of Greenwich Mean Time, in 1850, simplified analysis of recordings of weather systems which crossed political boundaries.)

The less precise aneroid barometer was left to draw its own record. The same mechanism that drove a pointer round a dial was easily adapted to draw on paper wrapped round a drum driven by clockwork. The charts are pre-printed with hour-lines and usually last for seven days. Vast numbers of such barographs have been pressed into the hands of retiring weathermen, mariners, agricultural scientists, schoolteachers and similar; they have been, and continue to be, a source of interest to both professional and amateur weather watchers.

Meteorologists sent lightweight aneroid capsules aloft to discover how pressures changed above the ground. At first small aneroid barographs were attached to tethered kites and balloons. Around 1895 the French instrument maker Richard made one such miniature apparatus which a kite raised to 1400 feet (426 metres). Aneroids went up on sounding balloons from the end of the nineteenth

This aneroid barograph made a dot each hour to avoid the friction imposed by a pencil held continuously against the chart.

century. In the years between the two world wars meteorologists began to build tiny weather stations consisting of thermometer, hygrometer and aneroid, with their own radio transmitter to send back coded signals. Observers on the ground plotted the balloon's track. On a free balloon the aneroid indicated height and as balloon soundings became more frequent it became possible to plot upper air pressure maps as well, essential for modern forecasting.

In Britain's Meteorological Office aneroids now supply the ground-level pressure measurements. Precision engineering and modern metals combine to make an instrument superior to most mercury barometers.

British meteorological stations now rely on these precision aneroids. The box expands against electrical contacts which generate an illuminated reading at the press of a button. Overall length is about 8 inches (20 cm).

ALTERNATIVES AND ACCESSORIES

At the same time that the mercury barometer made its appearance in the late seventeenth century, glass-blowers in Liège, in Belgium, were selling a 'weather-glass' for domestic use. This was a spouted glass container, often decorated with frills or mouldings along the sides or spout, which served as graduations. The glass was half-filled with water, but the space above the water was not, as in the mercury barometer, a vacuum. It contained air and water vapour, which expand and contract with temperature. The level of water in the spout was therefore controlled by both temperature and pressure. Known variously as 'water barometers', 'Liège barometers', or 'Old Dutch weather-glasses', they are still marketed on both sides of the Atlantic.

The search for portability led several nineteenth-century instrument makers to design something smaller, cheaper and, even if less accurate, handier at sea. Various old ideas were again considered which, with a better understanding of physics and new materials, were now practical. The most successful, judging by reports at the time and the numbers that survive, was Adie's sympiesometer, patented in 1818. The sensing element was a short tube containing hydrogen, above oil, the latter open to air pressure. As temperature affected the contents, the second element was a thermometer, from whose reading the scale was pre-set, and the pressure then read off opposite the boundary between oil and gas. Sympiesometers were made both as separate instruments and fastened on marine barometers. Later makers substituted different liquids and gases. The other pocket barometers gave less satisfaction and by 1850 had been defeated by the aneroid.

In severe conditions, on mountain or polar expeditions, the hypsometer was often useful. The higher one goes, the lower the temperature at which water boils. Armed with a set of conversion tables, the traveller unpacked his hypsometer, which consisted of a spirit lamp, water-pot and thermometer. Boiling some water, he noted its temperature and thus learned the pressure, which his tables converted to height above sea level.

Many barometers have additional instruments set in the case. A thermometer is by far the most common; temperature

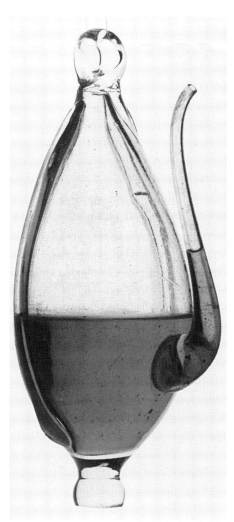

The 'Old Dutch weather-glass' or 'Liège barometer' has been made for sale since the eighteenth century and many examples, of uncertain age, survive in museums. Coloured liquid makes the level easier to read.

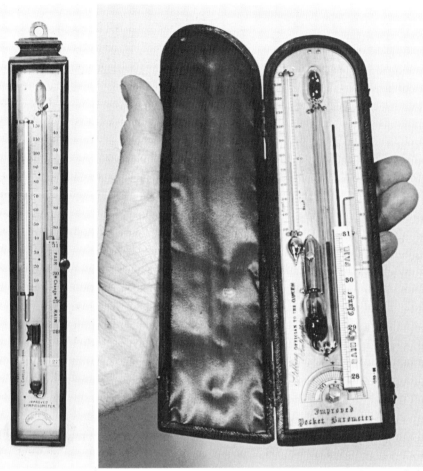

Left: *The sympiesometer, patented in 1818, was 'improved' by other makers. This example by Casella dates from the mid nineteenth century and is some 12 inches (30 cm) long.*

Right: *Stebbings's 'improved pocket barometer' was a scaled-down sympiesometer. These rather unsatisfactory pocket instruments were abandoned when aneroid barometers came on the market in the 1850s.*

observations were considered valuable long before the matter of correcting the barometer reading was recommended. The barometer reflected conditions out of doors, whilst its thermometer showed temperature within the room. Hygrometers, to measure humidity, were also popular accessories. Two forms, both known since the early seventeenth century, are found. One consists of a long twisted gut running down the back of the barometer. In damp air the gut untwists and lengthens; in dry air it twists up and becomes shorter. The lower end of the gut is fastened to the case, the upper end to levers moving a pointer round the dial in front of the case. The other form, smaller and cheaper, uses an oat-beard, the old countryman's hygrometer. With changing humidity the oat-beard twists

Above: *The hypsometer was a reliable alternative to the surveying barometer and was taken on mountain and polar expeditions until the early twentieth century.*

Right: *Twisted gut running behind the barometer case drives this hygrometer, graduated to show ten 'degrees' each side of average humidity.*

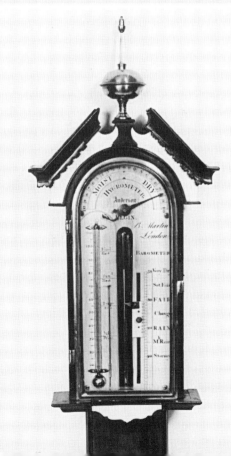

with sufficient force to drive a pointer round a dial. Banjo barometers often have oat-beard hygrometers. The 'farmer's barometer', related to the fishery barometer, had wet and dry bulb thermometers on its face, offering a more accurate humidity measurement.

Portable barometers often had a plumb-line and bob to assist with setting them up vertically and many banjo barometers have a little bubble-level fitted, for the same reason. Early nineteenth-century marine barometers may have a sympiesometer, making doubly sure that the captain was forewarned of storms or cyclones. Clocks, mirrors, lists of mountain heights and pressures, perpetual calendars and various homilies on the weather are more decorative than useful, but they were undoubtedly popular in Victorian times.

The barometer trade stands somewhat

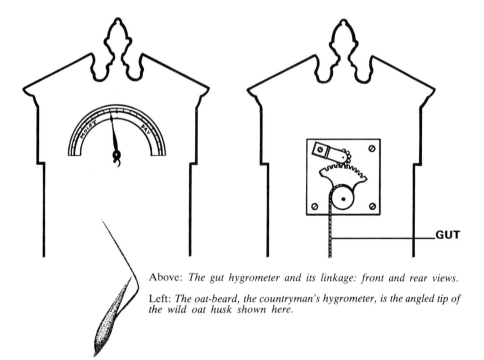

Above: *The gut hygrometer and its linkage: front and rear views.*

Left: *The oat-beard, the countryman's hygrometer, is the angled tip of the wild oat husk shown here.*

aloof from the manufacture of scientific instruments generally, having more to do with the cabinet-making trade. In Britain, some of the first barometers were commissioned from clockmakers: Daniel Quare, Thomas Tompion and Joseph Finney were notable clockmakers who constructed some extremely fine barometers. From the eighteenth century Italian craftsmen glass-blowers entered the trade in Europe and Britain, often working with local cabinet-makers. Italian names are found across the range of nineteenth-century barometers, some of these craftsmen expanding into other scientific and educational instruments. Eventually firms such as Negretti and Zambra were making vast numbers of barometers, anonymously, for export wholesale throughout the world. These were often retailed with the vendor's name emblazoned on their dials. The firm of Hicks cornered the market for aneroids, registering many patents for their improvement and in its turn wholesaling to other firms and shops.

Resident craftsmen at the observatories often assisted with the large standard apparatus, modifying and renewing certain parts over the years. The surviving apparatus may therefore differ considerably from its first form.

A good mercury barometer, in a decorative wooden case or a metal tube, is a fine instrument. It can also be a worthwhile investment, if properly cared for. Hang it in a well ventilated place, away from sunlight and direct heat. It suffers, however, from the passage of time, as well as careless handling; most barometers have undergone some restoration during their existence.

Where air can get to the mercury surface, dirt and moisture accompany it. The boxwood cistern probably presents the best defence, for leather cracks and sheds particles as it ages. The mercury oxidises, leaving yellow deposits against the tube, and rough handling lets air pass through the mercury into the vacuum at the top of the tube, so the barometer does not work. To check if this has

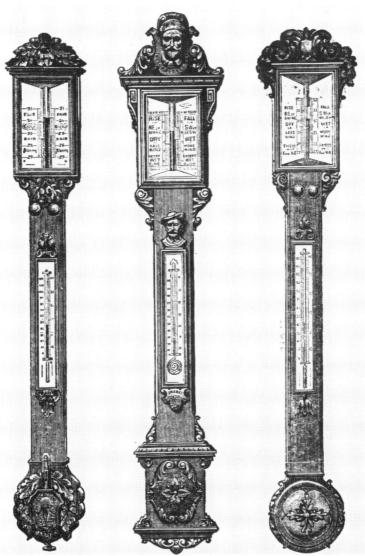

Lavish woodwork for simple barometers. The middle one commemorates (above) Torricelli and (centre) Drebbel, one of several claimed inventors of the thermometer.

95

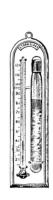

HICKS' OPEN SCALE BAROMETERS.

34. **Hicks' Patent Open Scale Baro-meter.**—This instrument yields readings in which a rise or fall of one inch of mercury on the ordinary Barometer scale is extended over a space of five inches to one inch (Fig. 19). £1 1 0

35. **Hicks' Patent Open Scale Baro-meter**, with a range of 10 inches to one inch of ordinary Barometer scale. £1 10 0

36. **Hicks' Patent Standard Open Scale Barometer**, on mahogany board with brackets, reading with verniers top and bottom to 1000th of an inch (Fig. 20). £4 10 0

37. **Hicks' Patent Spiral Tube Baro-meter** (Fig. 10), mounted in metal on mahogany board, with brackets, similar to Standard No. 1. In this instrument the scale is so open as to give 12 inches to one inch on the ordinary Barometer scale. £12 12 0

It will be seen on reference to Fig. 19 that the lower half of the tube is larger in the bore than the upper. When the column falls from the upper tube to the lower, it becomes shorter, and *vice versa*. It will thus be seen that by varying the relation between the diameters of the upper and lower portions of the tube, scales of any range may be constructed.

Fig. 19 illustrates an instrument in which a rise or fall of five inches is equivalent to one inch of the ordinary Barometer scale.

Fig. 20 represents an instrument with tube similarly constructed to Fig. 19, but mounted in brass tube divided from the centre upwards and downwards, with verniers to read at each end to the 1000th of an inch, the sum of the two readings giving the exact height of the Barometer at the time of observation. A delicate Thermometer is attached, to enable the usual corrections for temperature to be made.

19.
SCALE ABOUT 1·7TH.

20.
ABOUT 1·7TH

Above: *The barometer was an essential instrument for schools and colleges intending to set up their own weather station.*

Left: *Barometer makers patented a wide variety of scientific types in order to satisfy a growing and diverse world market.*

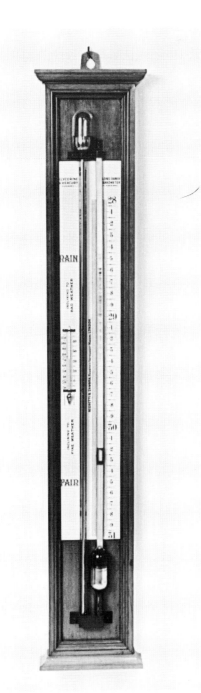

Inches	Millimetres	Millibars
31		1050
	780	1040
		1030
	770	1020
30		1010
	760	
	750	1000
	740	990
29		980
	730	970
	720	960
		950

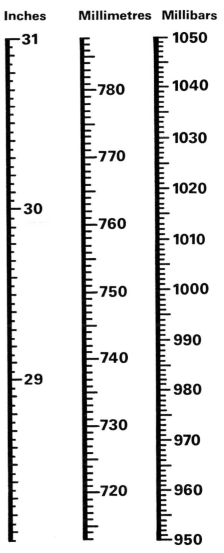

Above: *Conversion table for the scales most commonly found on barometers.*

Left: *Glycerine and mercury long-range barometer showing signs of age. The mercury column (left) is broken and corroded. Glycerine has evaporated from the right-hand column, leaving a dirty glass.*

29

Restoring barometers. With the glass and metal parts removed, the wooden cases can be repaired and repolished.

Several metals make up the delicate and complex aneroid box and linkage. The barometer will cease to work if the box is perforated or the linkage corroded.

happened, tilt the barometer gently: the mercury should fill the tube completely, giving an audible click as it reaches the top.

Barometers should never be moved upright without filling the tube and plugging an open cistern: if mercury surges in the tube, its weight may fracture old glass. Old barometers still in working condition have probably had new tubes at some time or times in the past. Bottle and complex tubes could not be cleaned and replacement was preferable to cleaning. The craftsman boils the mercury in the tube to drive out all the air, a practice which should deter owners from attempting to fill their own instruments.

The aneroid box, being extremely thin, may corrode and leak, slowing and then stopping its action. Frequently the linkage corrodes, which has the same result. Repairs are, however, possible and are worthwhile when the instrument comes from a good maker. Sympiesometers and other unusual instruments need the attention of skilled glass-blowers; the problem may be one of finding out what the original liquids or gases were and if they can be obtained today.

The best advice is: if in doubt consult one of the expert restorers who practise their craft wherever barometers and other scientific instruments are collected and cared for.

FURTHER READING

Banfield, Edwin. *Barometers*: volume 1 'Stick or Cistern Tube'; volume 2 'Wheel or Banjo'; volume 3 'Aneroid and Barograph'. Baros, 1985. These volumes are well illustrated.

Bolle, Bert. *Barometers.* Antique Collectors' Club, 1981. Written by a Dutch collector and restorer who shows the evolution of barometers and their accessories. Includes continental barometers.

Collins, Philip R. *Aneroid Barometers and Their Restoration.* Baros, 1998. Profusely illustrated; charts the development of the aneroid, with details of all types of aneroid mechanisms.

Goodison, Nicholas. *English Barometers 1680-1860, a History of Domestic Barometers and Their Makers.* Antique Collectors' Club, 1977. The best book for details of construction and for pictures of many royal barometers by the top craftsmen of the early period.

McConnell, Anita. *King of the Clinicals: the Life and Times of J. J. Hicks (1837-1916).* Sessions, 1998. History of the wholesaling business which manufactured numerous aneroid and mercury barometers.

Middleton, W. E. Knowles. *The History of the Barometer.* Johns Hopkins Press, Baltimore, 1966. Comprehensive and reliable survey of the history of scientific barometers.

Thoday, A. G. *Barometers.* HMSO, 1975. Small useful guide to the history of barometer development.

PLACES TO VISIT

Intending visitors are advised to find out dates and times of opening before making a special journey.

Barometer World, Quicksilver Barn, Merton, Devon EX20 3DS. Telephone: 01805 603443. The Banfield Family Collection of barometers.

Gloucester City Museum and Art Gallery, Brunswick Road, Gloucester GL1 1HP. Telephone: 01452 524131. The Marling Bequest Collection of domestic barometers.

Hampton Court Palace, Surrey KT8 9AU. Telephone: 0181-781 9500. Fine early barometers.

Liverpool Museum, William Brown Street, Liverpool L3 8EN. Telephone: 0151-478 4399. Scientific barometers.

Meteorological Office, London Road, Bracknell, Berkshire RG12 2SZ. Telephone: 01344 420242. Scientific barometers, to be seen by arrangement.

Museum of the History of Science, Old Ashmolean Building, Broad Street, Oxford OX1 3AZ. Telephone: 01865 277280. (Closed for refurbishment until 1999.)

National Maritime Museum, Romney Road, Greenwich, London SE10 9NF. Telephone: 0181-858 4422.

Royal Museum of Scotland, Chambers Street, Edinburgh EH1 1JF. Telephone: 0131-225 7534. Excellent collection, many by Scottish makers. Not always on display.

Science Museum, Exhibition Road, South Kensington, London SW7 2DD. Telephone: 0171-938 8110. Large collection of scientific barometers and barographs, not always on display.

Victoria and Albert Museum, Cromwell Road, South Kensington, London SW7 2RL. Telephone: 0171-938 8500. Barometers as furniture.

Wallace Collection, Hertford House, Manchester Square, London W1M 6BN. Telephone: 0171-935 0687. Barometers mainly by French makers.

Whipple Museum of the History of Science, Free School Lane, Cambridge CB2 3RH. Telephone: 01223 330906. Sometimes closed during university vacations.